GO-KART
RACING

BY JACK DAVID

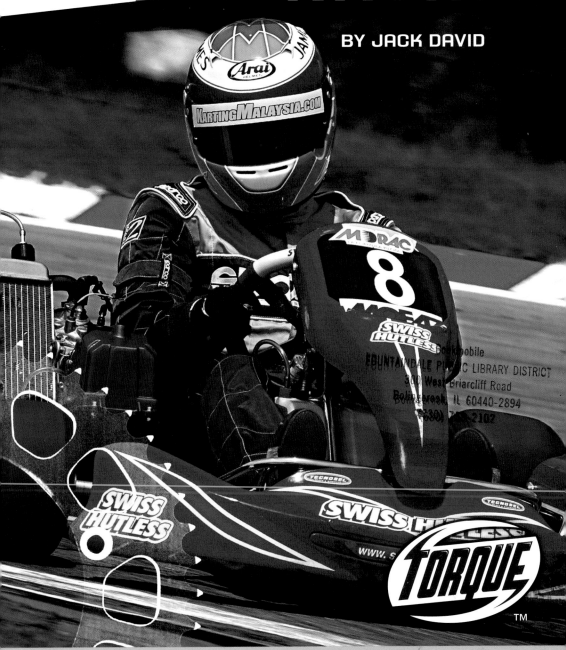

BELLWETHER MEDIA · MINNEAPOLIS, MN

TORQUE

Are you ready to take it to the extreme? Torque books thrust you into the action-packed world of sports, vehicles, and adventure. These books may include dirt, smoke, fire, and dangerous stunts. WARNING: Read at your own risk.

This edition first published in 2008 by Bellwether Media.

No part of this publication may be reproduced in whole or in part without written permission of the publisher. For information regarding permission, write to Bellwether Media Inc., Attention: Permissions Department, Post Office Box 19349, Minneapolis, MN 55419

Library of Congress Cataloging-in-Publication Data

David, Jack, 1968-
 Go-kart racing / by Jack David.
    p. cm. -- (Torque : action sports)
 Summary: "Amazing photography accompanies engaging information about Go-Kart racing. The combination of high-interest subject matter and light text is intended for students in grades 3 through 7"--Provided by publisher.
 Includes bibliographical references and index.
 ISBN-13: 978-1-60014-123-2 (hardcover : alk. paper)
 ISBN-10: 1-60014-123-4 (hardcover : alk. paper)
 1. Karting--Juvenile literature. I. Title.

 GV1029.5.D34 2008
 796.7'6--dc22

2007040555

CONTENTS

WHAT IS GO-KART RACING?   4

GO-KART RACING EQUIPMENT   8

GO-KART RACING IN ACTION   16

GLOSSARY   22

TO LEARN MORE   23

INDEX   24

WHAT IS
GO-KART RACING?

Professional race car drivers Jeff Gordon, Sam Hornish, Jr., and Michael Schumacher drive some of the fastest cars in the world. They all got their start racing go-karts.

Go-karts are small, inexpensive motor vehicles designed for racing on tracks. They are easy to operate, even for beginners. Many people see racing go-karts as a great way to build skills for racing bigger, faster cars. It's no wonder that go-kart racing is one of the most popular motor sports in the world.

FAST FACT

A basic go-kart can cost as little as $2,000. Many racers get better deals by buying used karts.

GO-KART RACING EQUIPMENT

Go-karts are small, simple vehicles. A metal frame called a **chassis** holds the driver's seat. The driver sits only about an inch (2.5 centimeters) above the track surface. Behind the driver is the go-kart's engine.

An engine's power is determined by its size. Engine size is measured in cubic centimeters (cc). Larger engines provide more power. Beginning karts have engines as small as 50cc. High-performance karts can have engines as large as 250cc.

Drivers can choose from two main types of karts. **Clutch karts** have just one **gear**. They can easily go 35 miles (56 kilometers) per hour. They rarely go more than 50 miles (80 kilometers) per hour. **Shifter karts** have five or six gears. The extra gears allow karts to go faster. They can reach speeds of more than 100 miles (161 kilometers) per hour.

Drivers must always keep safety in mind. They often crash into soft barriers around the track. **Spinouts** and even flips can happen. Rocks can kick up off the track toward a driver's head. Drivers wear helmets with face shields. They wear gloves, boots, and special racing suits to protect their bodies.

GO-KART RACING IN ACTION

Go-karts race on small tracks. A track can be a simple oval or can include many twists and turns. Most tracks are paved. Some karts race on dirt or even snow tracks.

Drivers can compete in a variety of races. Endurance races are the longest. They can last from 30 minutes to several hours. Sprint races are fast and furious. They often last just a few minutes. Speedway races take place on larger tracks built for bigger cars. Crosskart races are held on unpaved tracks. Riders are grouped by age and engine size in all kart races. This keeps the sport fair and fun for everyone.

FAST FACT

The top kart drivers can compete in the Karting World Championship. This event takes place in a different country each year.

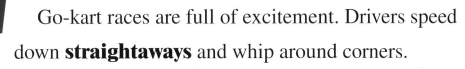

Go-kart races are full of excitement. Drivers speed down **straightaways** and whip around corners. The drivers are always battling for position. The leader tries to keep to the inside lane. This lane covers the shortest distance. Taking the inside lane also forces other drivers to pass on the outside. That is a tough maneuver. Everyone accelerates hard in the last lap. Fans go wild as they watch their favorite racer speed toward the finish line.

GLOSSARY

chassis—the metal frame of a go-kart

clutch kart—a go-kart with just one gear

gear—a set of wheels with teeth; the gears turn and transfer power from the engine to the wheels.

shifter kart—a go-kart with multiple gears

spinout—a sudden loss of tire grip, causing the back end of a go-kart to spin around

straightaway—a long, straight part of a racing track

TO LEARN MORE

AT THE LIBRARY

David, Jack. *Karts*. Minneapolis, Minn.: Bellwether, 2008.

Doeden, Matt. *Shifter Karts*. Mankato, Minn.: Capstone, 2005.

Herran, Joe, and Ron Thomas. *Karting*. Philadelphia, Pa.: Chelsea, 2004.

Savage, Jeff. *Go-Karts*. Mankato, Minn.: Capstone, 2003.

ON THE WEB

Learning more about go-kart racing is as easy as 1, 2, 3.

1. Go to www.factsurfer.com
2. Enter "go-kart racing" into search box.
3. Click the "Surf" button and you will see a list of related web sites.

With factsurfer.com, finding more information is just a click away.

INDEX

chassis, 9

clutch karts, 12

crosskart races, 18

cubic centimeters, 10

driver's seat, 9

endurance races, 18

engine, 9, 10, 18

finish line, 21

gears, 12

Gordon, Jeff, 5

Hornish, Sam, Jr., 5

inside lane, 21

Karting World Championship, 19

safety, 14

safety equipment, 14

Schumacher, Michael, 5

shifter karts, 12

slicks, 13

speedway races, 18

spinouts, 14

sprint races, 18

straightaways, 21

tracks, 7, 13, 14, 16, 18

The images in this book are reproduced through the courtesy of: Jaggat, front cover, pp. 3, 4-5, 7, 11, 13, 17, 18, 19; Juan Martinez, p. 14; Dyana/Alamy, pp. 6, 12; Paul Gilham/Getty Images, pp. 8-9; Pedro Jorge Henriques Monteiro, pp. 10, 15; Niall Day-Sawyer, p. 16; Margo Harrison, p. 20; Image Source Black/Getty Images, p. 21.